Also by Noah Warren

The Destroyer in the Glass

The Complete

Stories

Noah Warren

COPPER CANYON PRESS
PORT TOWNSEND, WASHINGTON

Cover art: Courtesy of Gabriel Warren

Copper Canyon Press is in residence at Fort Worden State Park in Port Townsend, Washington, under the auspices of Centrum. Centrum is a gathering place for artists and creative thinkers from around the world, students of all ages and backgrounds, and audiences seeking extraordinary cultural enrichment.

LIBRARY OF CONGRESS CATALOGING-IN-PUBLICATION DATA
Names: Warren, Noah, 1989– author.
Title: The complete stories / Noah Warren.
Description: Port Townsend, Washington : Copper Canyon Press, [2021] |
    Summary: "A collection of poems by Noah Warren"— Provided by publisher.
Identifiers: LCCN 2020047992 | ISBN 9781556596162 (paperback)
Subjects: LCGFT: Poetry.
Classification: LCC PS3623.A86475 C66 2021 | DDC 811/.6—dc23
LC record available at https://lccn.loc.gov/2020047992

98765432 FIRST PRINTING

COPPER CANYON PRESS
Post Office Box 271
Port Townsend, Washington 98368

www.coppercanyonpress.org

Contents

The Complete Stories

Wall Mice

There are two piles of documents: the one on the right
has to become the one on the left.
There is a paperweight in the shape of a whale.

Some pages have almost nothing on them, maybe
eight words floating in eggshell space.
They have to be read too,

so I do, I drift over them.

Once I used to wear a fancy belt buckle,
a cabin in cameo on a bright black field.
My left thumb would circle the oval as I wrote.

I miss that buckle. And I miss the dog
that slept in bed with us for six years, always nearer to me—you
curled toward the wall, me in the middle. I'd try not to wake
either of you when I got up at four to pee.

You were the slope of a shoulder,
the glow of heat beside me, and I could love that.

The brewery smell wafts in the open window, tangled
rot and freshness. Also jasmine, and cut grass.

When someone dies, their fears disappear
and the luster goes from their treasures
just like that. The accurate watch, the binoculars,
the stag-handled knife, the silver whiskey cup

that great-grandfather won at the county horse race in 1902
with a quick quarter-mile. Look what you've done,
it's your bed, said my mother

to my father, who was trying to get up
off the floor, reeking of Listerine.

A sharp rustling, like sycamore leaves
moving against each other.

In a previous draft, I was able to imagine you rising
to walk around the city at the same time I felt the need to walk,
or setting down a glass of water as I picked one up.

In a previous draft, I understood myself
as a man who preferred to write
on cocktail napkins, because they'd tear if he got too invested.
In that one, I kept my father apart from my loneliness.

You know this: there was a time
when I hung large silver gelatin photographs of glaciers
on the walls of my bedroom.
I was able to sleep like that.

They were my father's photographs. When I was small, he'd talk
for hours about the different kinds of ice,
about glaciers, and how they "calved." I loved that.
I could feel it. I felt the huge jewels falling into me.

Rustling Mind

You lay in the marram grass,

and read, and pedaled down to the wharf
at Havre Boucher where the salvage barge
hung groaning by its hawsers.

You sat on a bollard, you stared.
Gum in your stomach—

summer rotted away.

Night. You found yourself
walking slowly through your neighborhood.

In that window, you saw once
the perfect torso—smooth nave
of the rib cage, two small breasts.

That had never happened to you before.
You looked away.

And you fell into bed,
and if you dreamed, you dreamed
of the ark, vast
and charred as a star.

In the village story, the nephew
comes back in middle age, raises
the old Novak house and pours
a new foundation.
When it's set down, the floors
have warped and bellied, and the walls
lean skew. Not a door will close.

A kettle moans, you stir.
Mother smooths your hair.

Nous

1

He lifts the yellow backhoe
with the hoist he's rigged
to the I-beams of his studio;
it hangs in its chains like a bee.

2

On long tables, unarticulated
column segments wait to be welded
and planted in the meadow. Like teeth, they'll grow
brown with pollen, black with fog.

A decades-old Athena stares into the corner.
Her steel breasts and heavy legs barely
tacked—the idea of body, emerging
bitter from its matter.

3

He leans back wincing on his homemade creeper
and inches under the used machine.
Rust-bound casters screech—
his young assistant tenses.

He will wrench off the skid plate;
drain two trays of tarry oil; swap out
plugs, cracked hoses, gummed filters;
grease the housings; curse the pump.

For a quarter of an hour, though,
he just lies there,
a pocket flashlight clenched in his teeth,
testing lightly with his fingertips

the dark, intricate landscape
a foot above his face.

4

I remember the door banging open,
freezing the kitchen.
I watch crusts of sleet slide from
the toes of steel toed boots to the linoleum.

The linoleum is a dingy yellow;
likewise the Bakelite countertops.
A potbelly stove crackles, mutters.

He microwaves a bowl of carrot soup
until it bubbles, smothers it with vinegar
and grated cheese, shovels it down. He sucks
on his mustache for a minute

then marches out into midday again.

5

In the basement, under the red Bilco doors
two ricks are tucked, side by side:
one for the dried, one for the drying wood.
Depleted, filled, each few weeks their roles

reverse—so there will come a moment
when, uncurling from his battered chair
then creaking down the stairs,
sensation having faded from my toes

as the heat sank deeper in the stove,
I'll crouch squinting in that fusty dark
not knowing how to know which stack
I have to take from, when the sticks all feel the same.

6

There waits in a drawer a story that turns,
or grates, on words of love the father
has become unable, physically, to hear,
then say—

7

There waits, in that same drawer, the toy
the father helped the boy to build, to see him
through the winter grays. When the hull emerged
from its burl of maple, they named her *Pallas,*

like the real boat, and painted her the same: beetle green
above the waterline, Pompeii red beneath.
For that winter—the boy soon grew
dispassionate—the two craft were one,

and the arcing passage of the smaller
through the thin clouds around Block Mountain
brought the boy's heart to his mouth: as did tragedies,
the broken mast, the scars of Dog-Tooth Reef—

of which news informed, the mother, according
to her humor, could sometimes force a tear.

8

That year our house is finished. Unsalable,
the rock on which some other marriage
foundered, it had lain skeletal through a winter:
foundation, frame, plans, and tarps of lumber.

Daily my practical parents attacked it
with circular saw and sander and nail gun.
They camped in a tent, then the basement.
They were so young.

                    Ten years later,
nine years old, I watch my father hang its last
two doors—thin Z-braced tongue-and-groove—
on his bedroom closet. They swing silent and smooth.

9

One June he packed his tools and drove to a shack
in Canada. A tremendous lightness:
time fell apart.

It pooled beneath the trees we played beneath,
it wrapped the house like a cloud.

I swam across the big ponds,
Meadowbrook and Schoolhouse.
Pulling lazily at the water,
I learned to be tired. At night,

I lay naked on my narrow bed, I read
then masturbated then read again
my boring books as the sweating
ceiling slowly bellied down.

When the dog days came,
the whole house swelled—doors
stuck shut, and hundreds of tiny nails
lifted their heads from the soft pine floors.

Trash Day

Black rope it races
from the stones stops
between zinc bins breathes
then flutters
with its tender tuning fork
the heavy air.
I'm so tired. I remember
pressing a palm
then my child's cheek
to the cracked gray face
of Fox Glacier circa
1999. It was so big.
Now it's lighter. Snake,
I wish I wasn't afraid.
I wish I didn't have
to grope through shame.
My days come out to one
odd bag a week,
difficult to lift, always
I lift it in. Startling
you off.
        Somewhere
a rooster coughs. The ghostly
neighbor's put out
a ponderous knot
of wall chargers
and a walnut
dining set.
          I sit down
in walnut, I close
my eyes toward the crust
of sun burning through
the birch and its worming
mesh of shadows.

Wind

threw the pot of aloe from the balcony.
Bone yellow with a crackle glaze:
I was sitting close, I saw it teeter
on the railing,
the iron swaying—

There are so many plants.

On slender, ringed necks
the old palms whipped up and down,
and shone, and broke
on the wind.
The squat ones nodded.

I was wearing my hat and above me
a lake of blue fire. Volts of cream
came swirling off
the mountains, rushed across it,
and, twisting, tore apart.

I was walking up into the foothills,
I walked and walked. The day changed
in its sad, orange way.
I was unfree as the flowering pear trees,
unfree as the brown-cap birds tearing
the petals from their branches,
gobbling mouthfuls
of softness—

Warm rocks at my back,
valley in front of me. Oh valley

dark in the shadow, and dark in the light.

Operation Pedro Pan

Be not afeard . . .

This is the man with the tight black beard
that cascaded curling to his nipples.

This is the man with the strong teeth
and the belly laugh flashing full of teeth.

This is Aníbal, who in this country
called himself Rich. Rich,
who towered over me; Rich,
who arrived first, in a red Coke t-shirt,
and when they opened the hatch
onto a blizzard, laughed
and laughed at the sugar
spinning down; Rich, who vanished

into the mountains for a while,
and came back, and smiled;

Rich the careful, the claims adjuster,
the trembler, then the trembler,

gnawing his finger to remember
the *Tempest* prayer then in his rage

misting us with spit; this is Rich
with a scabbed vellum scalp
and his liver seeping diazepam,

the right half of his face white as cloud,
his dry lips slowly wrestling
around the clear tube—

Architecture

In the complex center, the field
where in the early afternoon
I would sit and rest. A broad
polished path of red-gray granite
cut it exactly on four sides, held it,
and no path led out or in;
here I would sit, the pristine
salad beside me, sensing
a forgetting taking place
lightly in the back of my brain.

The grass that filled this space
was of at least four different species,
not counting clover or the mosses
and so at any time
I might observe hues that ranged from whitened lime
to olive, to lustrous blue-green, to a deep forest
green so dark, when soaked or shadowed,
I took it for black. Each species grew
at such a different rate—St. Augustine fastest,
then bluegrass, bentgrass, and the wan fescue
(which dominated, or rather outlasted
these rivals on a sandy ridge
along the southern edge
where the topsoil had washed away)
painfully slowly—
that to make any sense of what I saw
I had always to recall that two
beautifully individual, if codependent, terrains
composed this visble landscape—
that barely perceptible, possibly original, south–north
gradient, with a spoon-shaped depression
in the middle, where I intuited a buried drain;
and, layered over it, the mesmerizing flux of blades
as they sought, as best they could, more light,
each blade wandering farther from the mean,
each blade full of chaos, compounding

its broken code
in the sun. As the sun
poured gold over the heavy stone
border that around me
lay still, precise, and empty.

Scarcity Theory

Warehouse district morphing into shops,
people building quiet lives, the wine importer
appends a retail experience.

I edited my tongue
until it was clean.

No—my friends helped,
I let them once I could read them;
tell me, I pleaded, opening
the cabinet of my face, what to cut—

A fig volunteered in front of Rainbow Market
and like a fan coral spread
up toward the constant flicker
of milk and beer insignia.

Have I improved at all? I imprudently
prayed in my notebook the afternoon
of my 28th birthday, after purchasing
the austere and mid-shelf Vouvray.

Carrying a paper bag, wearing
the sunlight like a crinkled cloak

down San Pablo,
that perfectly flat street

as my brain boiled pink flowers
and my phone tapped at my thigh
and my fingers crept over the glass
examining the light

discounts sent to me alone.

Novel

A feeling became dear

year buried in year
fox stashed in my cloak.

I named it *paragraph*.
A feeling became dear

melody, brother,
mind.
       The dog simpers

in his kennel,
poor idea.

This to keep you safe.
We loved each other

in a cabin on the lake.
You clawed my thigh,

bit at my nipple.
I named you *paragraph*.

I surrounded you with a life,
I named you *paragraph*.

I see these eerie muslin flounces
when I close my eyes.

Whole dresses folding
down into a cubic inch.

Novel

Who lies by the lake and hears high cloud ripping

Who undertakes another great project in the fall

Who changes partners

Who has eaten, all told, so much food

Who has been penetrated

Who has been not penetrated

Who travels to a student's funeral knowing no one
       and, because of a flight delay, arrives too late

Who has no thoughts whatsoever over a cortado

Who eats a bag of grapes a day

Who swallows grapes without ever chewing
       then shits them out, like little eggs, crumpled but whole

Who works two good jobs

Who always knows which drug, just how much, and from whom

Who finds a sense of purpose at home

Who rests like a dough

Who senses an eerie kindness glowing in the soft spring loam
       walking in the dripping woods for the first time in a while
       and understands, after an hour, how the dead do it

Who traces the rim, calm

Who decays out of kindness

Novel

Tom was everybody's ex. "He's an almost," everyone said, of William.
At midnight awkwardness passed from Ioanna to Leigh like a trophy.
Happy Hour morphed into Thrust and Parry Hour, Daniel versus Team Sloane.
Separately, fiercely, Eva and Min would bring up the day they hung out like friends.
A theory grew about love as a lobster, claws, meat, shell. I blamed Liz for that.
Summer brought assholes: some fun ones, but mostly Noreen and Laney's brother.
Gabriella and Chen, Ioanna and Bill, Tom and himself, too much Shane, Clara, *Annette*.

Novel

The first time he stared down a barrel it was his fingers cradling that clot of steel, and I do mean stare *down,* because he was sitting cross-legged, the pistol was in his lap, he watched both his thumbs flutter around the stiff trigger. It was very awkward. Through thin shorts, he could feel the pebbled grip press heavily against his dick. He was very awkward. He remembers the long whitish stalks of summer grass, swaying around him, broken under him, itching his shins and thick thighs. He remembers an overwhelming sense of boredom, and intuits now a lack of imagination that makes him pity that boy even more.

Water is colorless when seen from the air. Odd. The patches the eye sees grow baroque as they pass upside down through experiential knowledge, where they're woven into gowns for the heart. Reflecting, he decides he would cheat again. Reflecting, he sees he mistook the play he was in for seduction. Normal touch, it is said, reminds the body where it ends.

A limp quip begetting polite laughter begetting chimp laughter begetting a long howl of pain. Who will come and find him when he builds his cabin? Buds burst like bustiers on the twigs of May. Gravid elk strip the sapling apples. A clod of blue sky rinses his eyes. He *will* figure out how to make that borscht.

Say lines of plane trees mill the air into bronze. Of the accordions along the dusty boulevard, too few wheeze the boredom of summer light. The difficulty of comparing a strong, noble horse, with a jade, has wilted his courage. In a late twist, too late in fact, he will discover the troubadours were cruelly deceived about love.

A scraggly dun with high withers stares down the coast road, where rugged islets unzip the rolling waves. Above, light melts through woolen clouds. How could he be homesick? He has his habits. He lives inside them.

Calendar

Some waves came up overnight, though in Norderney, there was no weather.
At the commercial wharf, a thin stream of white exhaust rose vertically from the ferry.
The first service would depart soon. The puddles lay dark in the stone streets
and in the garden, and on the narrow walk. A bank of haze hung a hundred meters
offshore, perfectly still. While at the end of the long pier, the shallow-bottomed tjalk
that Tomas had restored, good at hauling, bad at sailing, knocked against the pilings.
It was regular enough that you began to expect the next knock
but then there was none, or two came quickly together and the effect broke.
Marta had been up before us, and made coffee, and laid out the table for breakfast.
A blue cloth, mugs, plates, and silverware, three zinnias in a thin white porcelain vase.
We helped ourselves to brown bread and cheese and the least strange-looking of the meats
she had rolled neatly on the tray. We ate quickly, gazing out the small window
at the blue and purple sky, the path down to the water, the long pier.

Abstract, Bio, Headshot

                        Snow
falling on the ocean,
snow in the redwoods.

And muddy streams streaming
fat down the steep hill. And the

deer, birds, and wild cats
appearing—then moving.

As days become us.
Once you pressed

the book that changed you
on me—disappointingly,

it was to be. You slit on me
a cut you called hot,

its warmth trickling,
your tongue extended,

lapping, your back arched
like a little dog, I said—

you stopped. And snow
slides from the green bough to break
on another bough, then another,

thirty-four degrees Fahrenheit,
the tone raw nostalgia,

the dialogue a wood: *Look at you,*
I said to you, and me—

you were looking
expressionless at me.

Jetty

The water shrugs, its heavy blindness.
Telephone wires scan and crease
cloud scud's bubbling lead,
their copper threads are empty now, web
of eerie interference, half-caught lyrics,
a sound like the ocean.

A sound like the ocean heard again
and again; a sound like a way of listening.
Salt drift drives through a puff of mist.
With the changing of the light
down the harbor boulevard
storms a torrent of quiet metal—

a metal torrent, which freezes
for another light, the cars magnesic
and pearlescent, sexual hearses like
black capsules of champagne.
They wait there steaming and red light
streaks them as if they were wet.

But they are not wet even after
this hour's rain; their shells forget,
and the eyes inside are the force of their forgetting,
lonely pilots. I have called you a friend
so we seem to both have lied
in service of a small idea:

small, silvering in the idea
did we lie together on a linen bier.
Not-us flowed through us, a thorn milk,
a blindness. When you swam from the world
I came with you. But you kept on; like mist,
you receded faster than I could.

If I lie, if I sleep,
I can still hear you receding. I listen
to the slender waves pulse the harbor

back and forth beneath small craft, never
strong enough to break, their force
gathered and relost.

Gathered and relost
between two gaunt long arms
of crushed stone.

Gina

In the lull after mussels, their oily shells
quiet as broken jaws, you'll roll
the stem of your glass between three fingers
so its foot wanders the cloth. It stops
and you'll frown at it, then raise
your face and say, "I miss the intensity
of friendship when we were young."

Crisp, cold, the wine fills your mouth;
hold it there until it fades.

The mains come: quail and sole. You smile
crookedly at a small thigh as you sigh it from its bone,
meaning, by the grate of your knife
against the square shale plate
that Gina left your life on a May morning
in 2013. She grabbed books from her shelves
as she spoke, threw some in a box, offered
you others. She was saying she'd married
the ranch hand so he could live
with her in Santiago. Her hands had paused.
She turned to look at you, she lifted her small chin.

That morning seems very long ago—her dachshund Henry
wriggling in her arms as you drove away, licking her lips.

Village

Cedar smoke wanders between the yards, past the linen hung out overnight

Max Ritvo

blinked at me from deep
behind thick glasses
as he thought. When he talked,
his commas were laughing flies.
Then he died.

Max Ritvo made his death
into a medium
of play and love—
like German.

I'm still intermediate in
Max Ritvo's death
but I'm patient.
Max Ritvo's death is worth it.

Cup of Snow

Statement—held
till it melts—
I'm sorry.
              Wrinkle of bats,
far croak of the chough.

The sun brushes the larch needles,
sweat beads a tiny copper kettle—

it burns my palm, it is cold
when I lay my palm on it.

In this room, three walls

of loosely plotted novels.
And a window. I could watch you

in the stone garden:
the carp fountain garbles
its frilled vowel

as you swirl your fingers
and raise a mist
of aqueous plant motes.

We stand facing each other,
or we sit in adjacent chairs,
and all the while, behind heavy doors
these spaces are seeding
further space.

There is a large walnut table, bowed
beneath the fiction of steaming food.
And there is a pale disk on the floor
where a lamp stood, that we step around.

Ants Swarming Bait

Three dogs on one leash, one
calmly peeing, in its clear
raincoat, the bare black tree
that blooms like a menorah.

Some have to carry sugar
back into the wall their nest fills,
where it will poison the eggs,
but most appear

to drink at the edge of the gel
until they fall still, and tilt
stiffly into the reservoir,
dissolving into commas.

Buildings

I see their streaked faces and recessed entryways, their windows
washed white by the rain. How cheerful, how brave
your voice was as you asked if I wanted anything from Whole Foods,
where you had to go, amid all the other Wednesday clutter—
turning back, you paused in the door, backlit by the morning gray.
Between us lay five years of love, which you talked about
as a quantity, that accumulates. And that morning was the beginning
of that night, morning, day, and night, those thirty-six hours
ten months ago now, when you convulsed with a new, raging sorrow
which I surprised you by returning, but more viciously, finding, as I broke
from the self I'd made, charring ecstasy—hours of weeping and reasoning,
of fucking, drinking, and takeout, hours of storming out and creeping back
and kissing dead lips once more to be sure, hours I refuse to remember
that hardened into the low city I walked out into, already retreating from me.

Hermit Thrush

After three years of silence,
oh.
    A grave

wound in the air,
a homeless

tongue:
Imperium

Constantini

scratched on a drop

of copper. I saw
man-sized

cells pock a ridge

where the hopeful
repaired to wither

and sing, their pupils
black suns.

Cold fills the throat
of the valley.

Patch by patch
the bark

slips from the oaks;

their pale skins
teem with food.

The song repeats

two times.

Letter

Thank you for the breams. William carried them over this morning, and besides
that they were large and shapely (as befits a stream so fair)
I commend you on their freshness—for tho I feared the contrary
when I beheld many droplets sprinkling and scattering from Wm.'s pannier
as he trotted up the rectory walk in this morning's sunshine, those droplets
were in no wise cloudy with corruption, but chrystalline, and ran rather
from the tight pack of wet straw your genius, or that of your delightful Mrs. Unwin,
had seen fit to devise. Poached in butter, brightened by that peppery cress
you once remarked upon, their flesh was sweet and airy in the mouth, and made for a lunch
(however *Romish!*) we'll joy to remember.

                                 The nature of our Father, and how our forms
of adoration prepare those of our reproval, have, I fear, been much in my thoughts of late.
My poor uncle Richard, whose acquaintance you made,
has succeeded in his long-held purpose. I mean that his body suffers no more, and I pray
that his soul find in time equivalent repose. I mean it was by his own hand he took
his leave, gulping down pills as Barbara, downstairs, watching first the fire,
then an entertainment, in time drifted off to sleep on the sofa.
It was a warm night. The windows were all open; village noises
and small, harmless insects wandered through the rooms.

In my fancy I see his soul, like a cranefly, or an admission of love,
blossoming from his lips. It circled once that room these past ten years
had confined him to, bade a brisk adieu to that scarred, papery corpse—
trembling no more—and then, downstairs, brushed Barbara's hair
with an awkward, delicate wing, by way of apology. For she has suffered greatly
his threats, his self-pitying rages, his jealous delusions. Indeed the details are so painful
that when we embraced, yesterday evening, I could not be sure
if we wept because her suffering had ended, or for the memory of Rich before—
his kindness, his infinite mirth—unclouded now by any recent present.

Calendar

Probably in another decade I will remember mostly the natural beauty of the cay,
which its nascent touristic development, the reason I was there, had not yet entirely effaced.
Such thought was however unavailable to me then, doubled over
beneath the banana trees at the edge of the island, retching with what,
in the lucid moments between spasms of deep skeletal pain
and the dry contractions of my guts, I was sure was cholera.
There were tiny fish skeletons and loose translucent ribs strewn about the dirty white sand
I was now lying on my side on, panting weakly, letting my head sink down on my arm,
closing my eyes against the stripes of sun that slashed between the blowing fronds.
Episodes of shivering occurred in different places of my body like earthquakes.
Forced to choose between suffering in the thatch-roofed eco-cabin I had rented,
which had no windows, or furniture except for the army cot, and was furthermore
infested by large, pulsating frogs that clung silently to the walls
and crawled to new positions when you turned the single lightbulb out,
and the beach, I had chosen the beach. Hiding my face in the crook of my arm, I could still hear
above the sloshing waves, the faint discordant tinkling
of the goats, or rather their bells, somewhere upwind. I had seen them climb
spindly palm trees, albeit bent ones, with an agility that made me incredulous
even as I witnessed it. They stood in the tops of the palms as if in the centers
of small green explosions, swaying around with the breeze, looking placidly at nothing.

Pistis Sophia

What is the nature,
the movement of that moment
in which I am still

recognizing you
as You? What force
fills the dark

torches of your eyes
as you lift them
from the essay you're moving

through, the Gnostics, the crisp
spring wind fluttering
the thin pages and a curl

your quick fingers tuck—

there is nothing the present,
welling from your eyes,
will not hold, nothing

it will not change.
It is a May evening:
we sail down to the street

for a cigarette,
to the seminary
where we lie down

on the lawn. We're staring
toward each other
then away, into the

night that reveals
itself slowly to be
already here,

and now our eyes are
close, and our mouths are

searching for the verb.

The Pity

How briefly I knew Greek! And by Greek
I mean the made rage
that made me slog back down that lizards' road
and—the guard agog to Turkish porn—softly
heave my pack then me over a wire wall.
I cut my palm. I slunk through the tunnel. I emerged
into the half-drowned theater and was cheered
by a key change in the mosquito-maenads' seethe.

I'd wrestled moods and Forms and rhetoric
as oak leaves fell upon Connecticut,
and attacked the weight gym as Snowpocalypse
retreated, as the dark earth fielded
myriad sharp stems; worshipful, confused
I'd got tattooed across my meaty spine
a doe-eyed bull with scimitarish cock.
I watched the needle in the mirror stitch
my mirrored skin like softly oozing silk.

Every evening in the bath Papa smoked and stewed.
Hard water drank his ruddy dirt. Tap tap the tips
sloughed gray into a faience dish.
Asked, he'd dart, "I was thinking about *you*."
His goaty thighs, his walnut skull, his face—

Such food I char for the dead.
For Abuelo I drizzle locust honey
around, then into, a small clay cup of rum.
For Abuela I scratch each saint's exile,
past and future, on banana leaves with an iron style.
Holy are self-martyrs; for her I gnash, tear, flee.

And is it *piety* that inflicts me, so ceaselessly
polite, on the quietness of exes' inboxes? and illuminates my heart
with pinpricks as I watch my mother's faces fail.

A thin road holds the cooling eye.
At the atom's center fizzes permanent exchange.
Sweating as I slept, guzzled like a wineskin,
I woke to doze in that drowned Asklepieion.
Birds crumbled dawn. Water snakes
crept over the swamp like script. I dreamed forever.

Allegiances

—Like so many fine twigs
snapped by the rainstorm
that's sweeping this city today,
heavy. It lashes the pastel houses
and the people walk by clutching
their jackets to their necks;
it looks like everyone is crying.

And I felt so bored and sad
that I dropped two threads of saffron
in the bowl of Cheerios I had for lunch
and that was a failure, obviously,
as I had been almost sure it would be,
the threads unable to blush the milk,
the oat flour turned soupy, the taste
just sharp enough to disgust me.

I stood at the window, I pressed
the puff cactus to see if its flesh
was still stiff under the pallid fur.
When I picked my fingernails,
the thin crescents fell and were lost
among the pebbles in the pot,
and all the older, curled-up parings.

Outside, the No Parking sign
and the bare school flagpole hummed
together in the gusts, pitched low,
a harp almost. They were safe—historical,
rooted in the concrete.

Once, the great struggle was between books and life:
between pattern and that terror,
that unfinishedness. Someone I grew to love
rested a hand on my shoulder and said—
voice careful with emotion—
"Your first allegiance must be to life."

It must have been winter then too:
outside, trees cobalt in the evening.

That room was too warm, small as a closet,
and every wall was lined with books of poems.
What a detail, I would think to myself later,
slogging home through the ugly snow.
Was that irony, I would wonder.

Blessing for the New Year

Three blue canvas coats, children, are returning from school
along a sidewalk dripping boughs overhang, the princess tree

the apple, and the persimmon, whose heavy fruits are all one color,
the color of its floppy orange leaves, which will hang

heavy as persimmons from the tree's jagged twigs
until a January storm takes them

or until new buds, swelling from the same soft spots in the bark
as they did last year, replace what was there with what it was.

Even relating it, Sofia shivered with the weirdness of it.

He'd read all my stuff online, I mean all of it. And he was like, glistening with the effort
of being nice to everyone, but especially me. How he knew I'd be there I don't know.
What I hate is that I bought it. I thought he was lonely, sure, but changed, mature. It was only
after, walking home, that Jen told me. And I yelled at her for letting me interact with that,
which I regret, but she fucked up. I don't care if he's sober: hate is worse. Hate is poison.
I'd been murmuring sympathetic words, my face mirroring her revulsion; now I filled my eyes
with the care I felt for her, and feel, however what I could find to say ended before the love did,
so a small silence came, Sam squeezed her hand, our expressions softened to the resting smile,
and as her head tilted toward his shoulder my eyes slipped over her other shoulder to
Miriam, who was putting down her seltzer because, I could tell, she was preparing to
talk, and as Mark was finishing, as everyone—Jasper and Rob, Mark himself, now me—
was still chuckling at his Folsom Street Fair bit, the leather grannies and the librettist
who played bemused but two hours later was getting fisted on the sidewalk, she launched,
drawlingly: That reminds me of the last time I saw John Ashbery: the National Book Award
afterparty was at an apartment on Central Park West, the elevator opened in the living room
and there he was, pouting under the chandelier, in his wheelchair, alone, he'd lost his handler
to the bathroom and no one was noticing him, so he just began waving his empty hand,
yelling *Gin and Tonic! Gin and Tonic!* And I tried, but there was only *champagne and elderflower* and
can you imagine telling that to *John Ashbery?*—Lord. It can ice your heart to rediscover
people you admired, or wanted to fuck, and find they're just the same. Across the room, I found
Molly's eyes and smiled. She didn't: she had opinions about Miriam, and so I made my face grave
like hers and, turning back to the circle to slip from it, saw Jasper's fingers on Mark's lower back,
which I was glad for: there are so few people. And it's uncanny how the deaths start so slow,
a few a year, even the terrible ones somehow logical, until gradually the shock grows constant,
or the unsurprise does, I don't know, it depends I think on whether you read life as a comedy,
the sustainable way, or as a tragedy, which according to Yeats is when we really begin to live,
I was saying to Rumur, post-bump, he was nodding, humoring me, when Lily broke in
Well I don't think how you read matters half so much as how you write, excuse me
for screwing up your metaphor, I mean how you live toward others; and I think some dissonance
between those is necessary, for art, sure, but also for intimacy—if that's going to mean anything.
I thought this was beautiful and I said so: her personal life, for four years, had consisted of flying
most weekends to Florida, going to hospitals, cooking, and helping raise her niece, as her sister died
of ALS. She smiled thinly and I knew I'd misspoken, I mean, this helps me, I said, that gap
has always haunted me, the silent self always judging out of pain, the self in the world fickle, trying
to make sense of what it's done, working to forgive itself. Maybe, she said, and it's true, vulnerability
often doesn't work, nor is it often true, Excuse me, I said, I'm getting signals from Molly, and I

went to her, because suddenly I felt small, and I loved her, and in each instant our problems still felt reparable, and were. I found her hand and she let me. She was talking to someone shortish, with cropped hair and a memorable face. She was saying that it's possible to recognize our limits for what they are, with bravery, even as we fail, hearing ourselves repeat the things we don't believe, and don't comfort us.

Two by Two

The thing and its spirit.
The foot and the wit.
The sweat of the brow,
wherefore and *how.*
The rifle, bridle, prick, peak.
Your forest eyes, that leak.
That warm North Face
gone "without a trace."
Not *8½,*
but Uncle Rich's laugh;
months of rain, neatsfoot oil,
leftover chicken in foil.
A *hecatomb.*
The middles of poems.
You, you, you, you.
Pokémon Red and *Blue.*
Jesse Owens's fist,
Dad's briefs in a twist.
Sim and Greta, Meena and Todd,
Campari, rosemary, ice, god.
Cliffs of flowering broom.
And what you assume I shall assume.
CBD and an embroidered coat,
the scurry of footnotes,
control.
            That hole.
Beasts clean and unclean,
birds, coffee, Dramamine.
The strangeness of time.
The grape, then the vine.

A New Landscape

presents itself. Large
and so soft a river

of scrolling silver
cuts it. Buildings intimate

city.
    I feel dizzy.

An esplanade occurs; its
willows.

      Boats like dragonflies
flicker up and down the bank,
through the broken shade.

—But whose is the dark
figure straying through
this papery air,

the sensitive intelligence
necessary to an October

evening?
    This way, come.

You descend with fin de siècle
courage to the current,
you swallow black wine

and close your eyes. Before you
the black wavelets crinkle
into sibilants

of assent; above you,
the leaves are leaves.

The leaves are also rain.

When it has been warm, cold sets in,
so you walk, someone beside you,

beneath plump white parapets
called "the wedding cake."
At a certain, curving moment

next to the memorial bench
filmed with dew, he stops.

A swan tears food from submerged stones.
He gives you half a smile

and a sad, swan-colored look. Oh,
you look and look. There are eyes
barnacled to the streetlamps, eyes
on cars, eyes climbing the air, eyes

behind the arrow slits; and a tier
of men behind each.
                                        The joke is
on them, of course.

He wants to fold you
into his huge houndstooth coat,
and he wants to fold into your hair,

into your little humming song;

but you're alone, dusk has fallen,
and its soft information
flits from an office in the cake.

Elsewhere, heavy fruit trees—
Venus lingering in a rain barrel.

At the bottom of your purse, your phone

soaks the mascara tube,
the brass and steel keys,

and a fresh packet of tissues
in glacier light.

Notes on the Mystery

Younger, I could go to my friend
when her heart had been pierced

and she was gasping for breath,
and I could tell her, nothing is lost

entirely, all experience
in time becomes a window.

She was twisting the wheel
of a wooden toy. I'd said more

than I believed.
Two blocks down, fine pins

of ice slurred the brackish water, slowed
the small waves, until on a last

heave, one
froze, a sheer shell

in the dark between the reeds.
When I search

my journals for her,
who melted from my life,

I'm searching for you, and for this
special faithlessness, I apologize;

there are so few people
in those soft covers, so many

descriptions of our four rooms—how they remain
the same, tall and old, quietly beautiful,

and yet change utterly as the sunlight
fills and abandons them on a clear afternoon.

Today was cooler. A high film of cloud
calmed me; a letter and an offer came.

Though I was tired, I brushed varnish on the floors,
let it thicken, then buffed it until it glowed

with cloths cut from a green flannel shirt
my father sometimes wore.

On Value

Late in the development of music,
a recorder echoed down the street.
Lopsided whole notes, B, G, C, C
left a fourth-floor window. It was
the kind of prettiness anyone could make,
the kind that everyone had.

*

When my grandfather died, a small black-and-white TV
entered our house. Alone in the house
after school, I crept down to the basement.

Snow.

Or, when QVC came through, a maze of grills,
perfumes, closet organizers, heart jewelry,
and solvents. "What have you been doing
all afternoon?"—"Nothing, reading."

A blue sewing table faced the window
in the frigid guest room, so whoever sat
sat with their back to the door, which, opening in,

concealed the gun closet too warped to lock.
On a low white shelf, the Library of America
through 1985. On the wall, a birthday card from Max Ernst

and that large, yellowing, girlish crow.

*

My grandfather's shortest long poem
inhabits Audubon to rediscover
the Southern landscapes, holy with grotesques,
my grandfather fled. Jean-Jacques's dark
Frenchness stands in for the intellect's
estrangement from its origins—whence
judgment—and yet, as Red
/Audubon learns, a cleaned gaze
curves back to the American sin
it composes, and stays.

This is also his best poem,
ending in utter candor: the boy self
pleads to the poet who inherits him,
"Tell me a story."

I'm in France for the fall—chimneys
thin as cigarettes, bright leaves

floating on the river.

A thin snow settles, melts.

*

Men beg

on the bridge a boy king
named for his mother—who held
his hand as he laid the first stone.

Fullness comes, then rhythm, and a sense of scale;
only then the line itself—if that comes.
It is that hope I would save.

Twenty-four,
ambitious, proud, that poet wrote
"The Briar Patch." He saw
in his South, an "image"—
as he glossed thirty years later,
very gently—"of the unchangeable
human condition, beautiful, sad, tragic."

*

Silence. Golf pencils, slips,
a slow clock. Page

two hundred sixty-four
halfway down, my finger

touches the spot
and I pull it back—

the words warm,
the sentence ice.

a deep grinding sound glass breaking
chariot wheels going by in the street below

*

Later he could not see
outside a shrinking circle in the center
of bright white blur.

Half his height, I took his hand, I led him
carefully down the path to the grove.

His face faced the ground.
Describe where we are, he said.

I would sound out the words
on his brittle lap, then he would

speak them smoothly, and I
had to read them again;

he pinched my wrist hard
when the accent was wrong, I

stopped, he whispered what I had to say
slowly into my ear and I said it

*

Sly earth tones, houndstooth, faux polar bear fur,
anonymity, the smell of urine and old iron, four priceless
lamassu looted, the ever-more-corporate FIAC,
two competing anti-FIACs, Johnny Hallyday's obsequies,
a terrorism scare, you, falling in an intersection while jogging,
my father forbidding me from coming home, on Skype
in his hospital bed, trying not to spend
a hundred euros buying boots, buying green lentils
carrots and tangerines "chez l'arabe,"
the loss of my notebook, freaking out, not you, the receipt
of a cryptic email about said notebook,
Rodger in the green suit, outside at the Esmeralda,
chatting easily, then vivisecting my poem.
—Artichoke, steak tartare.

Audubon is in the woods before dawn.
Gray becomes blue, and the sound begins.

As often as states enter the Union
he goes bankrupt; the frontier

evolving beyond him makes him
move Lucy and the children west, then west again.

He traces what he sees with a sensitive hand.
He tenses in his blind.

*

Vivid, shot, wired, dead, the ravenous
purple crow's crouched to spring

forward and gobble the two
creamy hummingbird eggs;
                                        dripping guilt,
he's about to hunch back into the gloss
of two hundred and three walnut leaves.

Winter light flickers strangely above him;
panels of spring sun burn into him;

in the summer I am not there.

Musée de la Chasse, Musée Cognacq-Jay,
Musée de la Conscience Blanche.

I was bright glass in your head,
a boulder in your heart.

                              *

Grandfather, a boy, lay down on the lawn
and fell asleep. Beyond the redbuds

his brother started arcing stones
over the redbuds, as high as he could.

The case I carry is small as a walnut,
old brass lined with green baize. Within

his glass eye pale as mine. He wrote
"Defeat is possible, and the stars rise."

Recorded Gregorian chant, real hammer blows,
a trumpet player with a voice like a cigar
muttering Greek into his phone. The barometer descends.
Someone I know is splashing Vantablack
across a marble torso. Someone I know
is in this room with me, observing me closely.
The river rises. Less than a block
away a long dove-feather gown is being sewn.
It has taken months; it will not sell.

The Complete Stories

Skirt leaves gone orange or torn away to reveal thorny branches, tops still flaming green
though their drowning climbed up them, the windbreak poplars glittered inverted
a moment on the flooded field until the clouds reknit. An empty road emerged
from the pools, almost touched the house. Quebec stretched to the horizon.

There were four of us but you were the one I passed the hours with.
In the long slow game, I bound you intricately to yourself with cotton ropes
and picked you up, and set you down on the carpet so I could nap.
The code is loose, therefore the sentence harsh.

Most of my life I would not believe the heart of life was making pasta
with a few people, sipping maybe two glasses of wine. In the evenings, when I was a child,
I played chess and backgammon with my father. To his credit, he never let me win.

We took a poll: most thought it was before midnight still. Talking can do that, make
a little time feel like a lot, or a lot a little, or both, in a way that makes
one feel pleasure, or loneliness, or a mix of these and many other emotions.

Notes

"Operation Pedro Pan":

Operacíon Pedro Pan (1960–62) was a clandestine evacuation of 14,000 unaccompanied children to the United States in the wake of the Cuban Revolution. It was organized by Father Bryan O. Walsh of the Catholic Welfare Bureau.

The epigraph is Caliban speaking in *The Tempest,* 3.2.135–43.

"The Pity":

An asklepieion is a temple complex associated with the Greek healer god Asclepius, whose cult was broadly popular in late antiquity. Patients would sleep on the temple grounds so that Asclepius might visit them in a dream, at which point priests would translate the dream into a therapeutic regimen. Theaters were common; the one in Butrint, Albania, is often flooded.

"On Value":

Jean-Jacques Audubon was born out of wedlock on his father's sugar plantation in Saint-Domingue (soon Haiti) in 1785. After the death of his mother, Jeanne Rabine, a chambermaid who may have been Black, his father brought him to France and formally adopted him in 1794. Confusion around his parentage was compounded by the false passport with which he immigrated to the United States in 1803, contributing to the persistent rumor that he was "the Lost Dauphin."

The crow referred to is *American Crow,* plate 156 in *The Birds of America* (J.B. Chevalier, 1844).

The long poem in question is Robert Penn Warren's *Audubon: A Vision* (Random House, 1969).

The reader is referred to the collection of essays *I'll Take My Stand* (Harper & Brothers, 1930). Warren's contribution, "The Briar Patch" (246–264), advocates for a segregated agrarian economy. It summarizes: "Let the Negro sit beneath his own vine and fig tree" (264). Warren would later recant this essay and its positions as his politics shifted to the left. A series of 1964 interviews with leaders of the Civil Rights Movement were gathered into *Who Speaks for the Negro?* (Random House, 1965).

Acknowledgments

I am grateful to the editors of the following publications, in which these poems first appeared, sometimes in different form:

AGNI: "Jetty"

The American Poetry Review: "Novel" [The first time he stared down a barrel . . .]

The Cincinnati Review: "Cup of Snow"

Five Points: "Buildings" and "Trash Day"

Literary Imagination: "Letter"

Literary Matters: "Buildings"

New England Review: "A New Landscape"

The Paris Review: "Allegiances," "Calendar" [Some waves came up overnight . . .], and "The Complete Stories" [Even relating it . . .]

PEN Poetry Series: "On Value"

Ploughshares: "Wall Mice"

Poetry: "Notes on the Mystery"

The Sewanee Review: "Architecture" and "Nous"

The Southern Review: "Blessing for the New Year," "Rustling Mind," and "Wind"

Subtropics: "Hermit Thrush"

"On Value" was reprinted in *Salon de Belleza* (Wolfman & Gato Negro, 2020).

I owe Eavan Boland a great debt for her generosity, and I mourn her passing. My deepest thanks to Christina Ablaza and the Stanford Creative Writing Program for their support.

Of many friends and mentors at UC Berkeley, I bow especially to Lyn Heijinian, Geoffrey G. O'Brien, Charlie Altieri, Kevis Goodman, Elisa Tamarkin, Eric Falci, and Sam Otter.

To the James Merrill House Committee, for time and hospitality.

Thank you, Michael Wiegers, for giving this book a home. Thank you John Pierce, Elaina Ellis, Laura Buccieri, Emily Grise, and everyone at Copper Canyon Press, for taking such good care of it.

*

To those whose read, edited, informed, challenged, and changed this book, whether they knew it or not:

Richie Hofmann, Will Brewer, Brian Tierney, Jessica Laser, Edgar Kunz, Grady Chambers, Sam Ross, Alex Dimitrov, Katie Peterson, Nate Klug, Margaret Ross, Daniel Poppick, Danniel Schoonebeek, Devon Walker-Figueroa, Justin Boening, Kit Schluter, Jesse Nathan, Ryann Stevenson, Christian Gullette, Christian Schlegel, Jared Robinson, Leo Dunsker, Lindsay Choi, Randall Mann, Kai Carlson-Wee, Matt Siegel, Michael Shewmaker, Ari Banias, Jordan Zandi, Hannah Zeavin, Hannah Loeb, Emma Catherine Perry, David Gorin.

Jacob Albert, Will Chancellor, Ben Hoffman, Chris Drangle, Stephen Sparks, Roman Muradov, Rumur Dowling.

Louise Glück, Rosanna Warren, Rodger Kamenetz, D.A. Powell, Henri Cole, David Ferry, Carl Phillips.

i.m. Max Ritvo. i.m. Richard Flores.

Ana, Gabriel, Sofia.

About the Author

Noah Warren's first book, *The Destroyer in the Glass* (2016), was chosen by Carl Phillips for the Yale Series of Younger Poets. A former Wallace Stegner Fellow, he lives in Oakland, where he is pursuing a PhD in English at UC Berkeley.

Poetry is vital to language and living. Since 1972, Copper Canyon Press has published extraordinary poetry from around the world to engage the imaginations and intellects of readers, writers, booksellers, librarians, teachers, students, and donors.

Copper Canyon Press gratefully acknowledges the kindness, patronage, and generous support of Jean Marie Lee, whose love and passionate appreciation of poetry has provided an everlasting benefit to our publishing program.

WE ARE GRATEFUL FOR THE MAJOR SUPPORT PROVIDED BY:

THE PAUL G. ALLEN
FAMILY FOUNDATION

 amazon *literary partnership*

4 CULTURE

 the **point**
envision·enact·evolve

Lannan

 **ART WORKS.** | National Endowment for the Arts
arts.gov

 A&
OFFICE OF ARTS & CULTURE
SEATTLE

 WASHINGTON STATE
ARTS COMMISSION

TO LEARN MORE ABOUT UNDERWRITING
COPPER CANYON PRESS TITLES,
PLEASE CALL 360-385-4925 EXT. 103

WE ARE GRATEFUL FOR THE MAJOR SUPPORT PROVIDED BY:

Anonymous

Jill Baker and Jeffrey Bishop

Anne and Geoffrey Barker

In honor of Ida Bauer, Betsy Gifford, and Beverly Sachar

Donna and Matthew Bellew

Will Blythe

John Branch

Diana Broze

John R. Cahill

Sarah Cavanaugh

The Beatrice R. and Joseph A. Coleman Foundation

The Currie Family Fund

Stephanie Ellis-Smith and Douglas Smith

Laurie and Oskar Eustis

Austin Evans

Saramel Evans

Mimi Gardner Gates

Gull Industries Inc. on behalf of William True

The Trust of Warren A. Gummow

William R. Hearst, III

Carolyn and Robert Hedin

Bruce Kahn

Phil Kovacevich and Eric Wechsler

Lakeside Industries Inc. on behalf of Jeanne Marie Lee

Maureen Lee and Mark Busto

Peter Lewis and Johnna Turiano

Ellie Mathews and Carl Youngmann as The North Press

Larry Mawby and Lois Bahle

Hank and Liesel Meijer

Jack Nicholson

Gregg Orr

Petunia Charitable Fund and adviser Elizabeth Hebert

Gay Phinny

Suzanne Rapp and Mark Hamilton

Adam and Lynn Rauch

Emily and Dan Raymond

Jill and Bill Ruckelshaus

Cynthia Sears

Kim and Jeff Seely

Joan F. Woods

Barbara and Charles Wright

Caleb Young as C. Young Creative

The dedicated interns and faithful volunteers of Copper Canyon Press

The Chinese character for poetry is made up of two parts:
"word" and "temple." It also serves as pressmark for
Copper Canyon Press.

The poems are set in Adobe Garamond Pro.
Book design and composition by Phil Kovacevich.